DUPAIN'S AUSTRALIANS

Previous page: Charlie South, model maker – 1950s   Above: Globe Hotel, Toowoomba – 1946

DUPAIN'S AUSTRALIANS

TEXT BY FRANK MOORHOUSE

JILL WHITE

CHAPTER & VERSE

Above: Anniversary day regatta from Bradleys Head – n.d

Opposite: Bankstown boys don't cry – 1932

First published in 2003 by Chapter & Verse, an imprint of Wellington Lane Press Pty Ltd, 120 Wycombe Road, Neutral Bay, NSW 2089 and John Witzig & Company Pty Ltd, Mullumbimby, NSW 2482.

Copyright © 2003 Chapter & Verse.
Text © Frank Moorhouse
Photographs pp. 63, 66, 67, 69, 70 and 86 © Max Dupain & Associates, used with kind permission.
All other images © Jill White.

Edited by Carol Dettmann. Designed by John Witzig.
Photographic edit by Jill White and John Witzig

National Library of Australia Cataloguing-in-Publication data:

Dupain, Max, 1911-1992.
Dupain's Australians.

ISBN 0 947322 26 4.

ISBN 0 947322 28 0 (Limited ed.).

1. Dupain, Max, 1911-1992. 2. Portrait photography - Australia. 3. Australians - Portraits. I. Moorhouse, Frank. II. White, Jill. III. Title.

779.092

Printed in Singapore by Kyodo Printing Co.

Photographic paper for exhibition prints was generously subsidised by Agfa-Gevaert Limited.

AGFA

Publication of this book was made possible by the generous support of Perpetual Trustees Australia Limited and W9&10, a joint venture company owned by Multiplex & Australand

CONTENTS

CRAFT, NOSTALGIA AND KEYHOLES – THE THREE-PART GAZE

FRANK MOORHOUSE

Tell me what you see vanishing, and I
Will tell you who you are. – W. S. Merwin

When the publishers suggested I might write the introduction to *Dupain's Australians*, I asked which period the photographs covered, and was told mainly the 1930s and 1940s.

I said, 'Of course I'll write it – that's my period.' The 1930s and 1940s are not when I *lived* but are a period that I felt I *knew*. I had written three books, a novella and a film about those years.

For Max Dupain (1911–92) these years were when he was in full-flight as a man and as a professional photographer. He began work as a photographer in 1929 as an eighteen-year-old and by the time World War II began he was married to his childhood friend Olive Cotton, also a photographer.

Most of us living now come to his photographs of the 1930s and 1940s with a three-part gaze. The first part of this gaze sees the art of his work, his individuality, and I wish to return to that.

The other two ways of seeing which we bring to bear would have irritated Dupain – they are the gaze of *nostalgia* and what I call the gaze of the *keyhole*. The word nostalgia is from the Greek word *nostos* which means 'to return home' but for most of us nostalgia is not precisely a 'return home' but a more delicate, difficult-to-define relationship.

Looking at the photographs in this book at this particular time in history, we experience nostalgia – that pleasing sense of looking again at what we remember but which has now changed: a regretful or wistful memory or a yearning for our past. The images bring to our mind the words, 'I remember that!'

Nostalgia is often considered a lower-order aesthetic experience, a shallow engagement with art, which belongs with older people. To experience nostalgia you need something to look *back on* – time has had to pass and the more it passes the more frequent nostalgic experiences become.

Perhaps we give it a low status in our sensibilities because we live in a forward-looking society that overvalues change: nostalgia is seen as an unproductive 'backwards looking' consciousness, a sentimental rejection of modernity.

Evidence of its low status is nicely expressed by the editor of *Light Vision*, a photographic magazine that in 1978 published a small retrospective of Dupain's photographs from the 1930s. The editor said that

publication of the photographs must not be seen as an 'indication of a desire to succumb to the attraction of "nostalgia"'.

Dupain used the word in his introduction to *Max Dupain's Australia* (Penguin, 1986) describing, rather sarcastically, the selection of photographs as having '…a large dose of nostalgia thrown in for its soothing effect'.

Nostalgia is not always a soothing experience. It can produce rage at things unnecessarily destroyed and pain from a sense of irretrievable loss.

If we choose to initiate it, nostalgia presents to our mind a chain of existential questioning. Questions about preservation and renewal, about loss and evolution, about the inevitability of change, about resisting change, about 'newness' and value. What has really changed? Have we really advanced on that which our parents and grandparents had? Why were our immediate relatives the way they were? Why did they think so differently from us? Why did our parents not *realise* or *know* what we know? Or conversely, why sometimes do we see their time as being solid, more coherent, more authentic?

The other consciousness closely related to nostalgia, which these photographs evoke among many of those living now, is what I call the *keyhole gaze*.

The Keyhole

As well as offering us the experience of nostalgia, the photographs in this book are also a keyhole through which we can look into our parents' life and times (and with the nudes, something of a peep into their bedroom – which the psychiatrists would say is our ultimate curiosity).

This is different from nostalgia.

Nostalgia allows us to see the lost world which we, in part, experienced – 'I-remember-that' – but the keyhole gaze allows us to see the world *just before we were born* – how the world was just before we arrived in it. Dupain had the eyes of our parents' generation and, because he was a photographer, he is *our* eyes, is our way back to that time.

This pre-birth time is of critical interest to humans and it is only with photography that we are able to experience it visually. There were paintings and sketches and verbal descriptions of the time before we existed but not all had access to them. For the first time in human history, the photograph gave most people an easy and cheap physical record of personal images and an acute access to both the nostalgic and the pre-birth worlds.

Opposite: Spontaneous composition – 1935

Of course, many traces of our parents' life – buildings and so on – also overlap with our existence. But in the ever-changing nature of contemporary life, these traces are gradually erased by the passing of time, especially in the New World before heritage-consciousness raised the value of preserving 'examples' and facades from the past.

So buildings are demolished, businesses close or change names, products disappear (sometimes the billboard advertisements for bygone products are revealed and give off a special nostalgia), street patterns change, and unlike more traditional societies each generation tries to *look* different from its parents in its clothing and in its styles (although sometimes fashion surprisingly returns us to our parents' or grandparents' world).

And those of us who view these photographs with these ways of seeing are given a special relationship to the photographs, a gift of our age, our placement in history.

We will also be the only generation to see these images this way. Other generations cannot have the same time-relationship to the photographs that we have, that is, of being of our parents' time and of depicting things – buildings etc. – that we have shared with the Dupain of the 1930s and 1940s.

Future viewers will see the photographs as historical documents without the personal patina that we experience – there will be no memory link.

The more we think about it, *time* ultimately – in fact, very quickly – becomes a co-subject of every photograph. Time changes our relationship to every photograph as it does of course in a more general way to all art – to what we take from art and what we look for in it.

Sources of the Dupain aesthetic

I suspect Dupain would have been irritated by my dwelling on and elaboration of these two types of *seeing*. For nostalgia and keyhole vision the *subject* is everything. Max Dupain wanted us to see the *craft* of his photographs. But we can see that as well. One gaze does not necessarily exclude another.

I approach the question of Dupain's aesthetic with three inquiries in mind. What social or political implications are there in the work, intended or inherent? And why did Dupain choose a particular subject and why did he compose a photograph as he did?

There were many more 'philosophies' or creeds and ideologies (wide arching all-explaining theories) in Dupain's world than in our own – Imperialism, Nationalism, Fascism, Communism, and Freudian theory. These have faded and we have come to treat ideologies or Master Theories as suspect.

Can we find an expression of any coherent body of ideology in the work of Dupain? Or is he perhaps *sans doctrine,* which was how the French visitor Albert Métin once described Australian socialism?

On one level we know certain things about Dupain's thinking – during World War II he stated he was a pacifist and wouldn't even consider covering the war itself as a photographer. However, he lent himself to the war effort through the camouflage unit.

At times he stated that he was an atheist and he would almost certainly have been a supporter (but perhaps not a member, I bet he was one of those people who say 'I am not a joiner') of the then flourishing Sydney Rationalists' Association whose stated position was the adoption of 'those mental attitudes which unreservedly accept the supremacy of reason' and which aimed at establishing 'a system of philosophy and ethics verifiable by experience and independent of all arbitrary assumptions or authority'.

We can find disdain for the monarchy in his republican remarks about the 1956 royal visit being a 'circus' – although he photographed it.

One belief from Dupain's world which has gone from our vocabularies (but not from some contemporary thinking, couched in new words) was called Vitalism. This doctrine holds that living organisms possess a non-physical inner force or energy, a notion of a 'vital force' or 'life force' which transcends the laws of chemistry and physics. Gael Newton, a major Dupain expert and curator of photography at the Australian National Gallery, feels that influences of Vitalism can be found in Dupain's personal world and in his photographs. D. H. Lawrence (who Dupain read and admired) and the painter Norman Lindsay (whose work and writings influenced the young Dupain) were proponents of Vitalism. Though Dupain made no statement about his attitude to Vitalism, it would have been in his consciousness.

Sebastian Smee says in his introduction to *Dupain's Beaches* (Chapter & Verse, 2000) that Dupain saw in sport 'affirmations of virility and the masculine "life force"'. For example, Dupain saw surf carnivals as 'a parade of masculinity' and as typifying Australia. And *Discus* – 1937 (p. 55) has faint echoes of the communist and fascist aesthetic – but is not a photograph typical of the Dupain work I have seen.

Vitalism was also connected in Australia with athletics and gymnastics. Dupain's father George was no doubt an important influence on his son, with his gymnasiums and his emphasis on physiology and nutrition. Even the bushwalking movement at this time reflected this belief with its mild spiritualism through nature and the spiritual 'health' which supposedly came from strenuous activity out in nature. Vitalism is found in the codes and handbooks of many youth movements in the 1920s, 1930s and 1940s. These were the times of popular patriotic youth movements such as Boys' Brigade, Boy Scouts, Girl Guides, British Empire Youth, Red Cross Youth and many others, which often had marching bands, insignia, ceremonials, uniforms and flags. Women had their own sort of 'life force' in that culture.

Vitalism has for us now an unpalatable connection with hygiene and fitness combined with ideas of 'purity' of blood and virile or macho behaviour.

Perhaps his father's influence caused an early interest in this area (Dupain did many male nude studies which echoed the illustrations on the walls of his father's gym) but he later developed his own attitudes. Try as I might, I can't really find strong traces of Vitalism in these photographs by Dupain – or for that matter evidence of any of the potent ideologies of his day. In some of his work I was reminded of Henry Lawson's identification with 'the people', a mild form of humanistic populism – a belief in the 'goodness' or even wisdom of the non-intellectual mainstream perhaps, and a concern for the less fortunate.

Meat queue – 1946

Lawson's verse and stories would have been known to every Australian of Dupain's generation.

Dupain's preoccupation with the 'faces in the street' through his many photographs of people in public spaces – travelling in ferries and trains, on beaches, walking in the street, audiences, crowds, and especially queues – perhaps reflects a Lawsonian populism.

These photographs bring to mind the words of Lawson's poem 'The Faces in the Street':

> *In hours before the dawning dims the starlight in the sky*
> *The wan and weary faces first begin to trickle by*
> *Increasing as the moments hurry on with morning feet*
> *Till like a pallid river flow the faces in the street –*
> *Flowing in, flowing in*
> *To the beat of hurried feet –*
> *Ah! I sorrow for the owners of these faces in the street.*

But Lawson's humanism seems to me somewhat melancholy, while one critic said that Dupain's photographs 'lacked angst' and Dupain himself wrote that his work 'reflects the rather wonderful life I have enjoyed as an Australian…'.

Did Dupain really believe that his photographs made people 'think' as he often stated that photography should? This is a humanist position implying not that the creator is necessarily pushing a position (or at least not a position that is revealed), but that he or she thinks people are accepting prevailing conventional beliefs that they should question and perhaps discard. Dupain implied that the photograph was an invitation to inquiry but I suspect this was itself a dutiful and wishful adherence to humanist values.

Photographs can focus us on subjects and cause us to see with clarity, show us our surroundings in a way we had not seen them, or it can awaken our awareness (as in war photography). But to hope that photographs will cause people 'to think' is a rather forlorn expectation of a

Waiting for the main event – 1938

photograph unless it is a spin off from special ways of seeing which I have outlined earlier or those graphic illustrations of world crises such as war.

The central tenet of Dupain's craft aesthetic was that the subject is nothing, the light is everything.

Dupain said that he wished for people to see his photographs as 'photography' – that is, to disregard the subject, at least after the first viewing, and to see the artfulness of it which is what he thought should be the primary *subject*, that is, the beauty or strangeness or specialness of the photograph as *photograph* – his working with tonality, light, composition 'manoeuvring the view point' and pattern.

That is why Dupain would have been irritably restless at my dwelling on nostalgia or on the quality of iconography which place the surface subject in a primary position (at least as the first response).

Throughout his life, Dupain mainly stayed with black and white photography. At first, black and white photography was a technological limitation on the art of photography and was the first and most fundamental aesthetic break by photography with 'realism' – there was in a sense no visual 'realism' in photography until colour. Photography artificially changed the world into black and white.

Dupain made a decision to continue to use black and white film and its creative artificiality, that is, its reduction of the world to a place without colour. He did publish some of his colour work in the book *Dupain's*

Bondi – 1939

Australia. But in a TV interview he said that 'colour [photography] was at a stage where it depicts so objectively that nothing is left for individual interpretation, colour is not interpretative, you get sick of seeing a colour photograph again and again. Black and white is the inherent photography, it has it "all over" colour...'.

Finally, for me, Dupain's photographs of people are characterised by a recessiveness. They are never risqué, nor do they venture into highly sensitive places (as in the work of say, Sally Mann and Bill Henson, which visits the sexuality of adolescence), they do not record deformity or the physically marginalised (as in the work of Diane Arbus) nor is there any use of distortion by lens or other means (except in the Man Ray-influenced shots from his early days). Dupain photographs never show anything like the intrusion of the American photographers William Klein or Gary Winogrand, with hostile confrontation between subject and photographer; there are no startled and antagonistic subjects in Max Dupain's images.

There are rare 'stolen moments', even the beginnings of a voyeuristic eye such as the classic photograph *Bondi* (1939) of the woman adjusting her swim suit, but there is no consistent pursuit of aggressive or persistently intrusive *caméra verité* and no evidence of a persistent voyeurism.

Maybe Dupain's work could be described as almost a *shy camera*.

In his aesthetic there was a degree of 'arrangement' and manipulation of the negative, a manoeuvring of his point of view and a strategic timing of the light for maximum contrast, but the evidence is that Dupain did not go in for dramatic 'setting up' of his photographs (as in the theatrical staged work of Tracey Moffatt, Jeff Wall and Cindy Sherman who create 'scenes' and play with popular culture images).

Dupain's reality is an ordered and now mellow normality. In his photography, Max Dupain never went anywhere he shouldn't be (except unintentionally by giving us something of a keyhole on our parents' generation).

The creative uses of chance

In the case of the woman in the rayon swimsuit in *Bondi* (1939), Dupain said that *luck* or chance played a part.

Dupain said that he had already photographed the couple from behind and from a low angle and felt he had a strong photograph but he had the alert perceptiveness of an artist which kept him watching just a little longer, to be presented with the next photograph – of the woman pulling the swimsuit down over the cheek of her buttock. What Dupain would have instantly recognised was that this pulling down of the swimsuit by the woman was something he had unthinkingly seen over his years at the beach. Suddenly this common but furtive human action was there and he caught it.

Implicit too, is the evidence that the woman who is watching something to her front with the man was, at the same time, in another part of her mind, conscious of her appearance to someone viewing her from behind.

More stunningly creative chance has played a huge part in creating the iconic *Sunbaker* (1937) [see p. 22]. Dupain's first choice among the negatives of the *Sunbaker* shots, published in 1948 (the negative is now lost), is not as fine as the second choice which was not published until 1975 (the poster image of the first retrospective at the Australian Centre for Photography in Sydney). The selection by Dupain of the first print seems to represent a lapse of judgement, but luck gave him the chance to select a second time.

Dupain often refers to luck. It may have been deprecation of his art but it is also a part of art.

Luck or chance in art comes in a number of categories. There is the *aleatoric* – random choice deliberately introduced by the creator – say, the throwing of a dice, or its equivalent, to decide an artistic act. In writing there was for a time something called the cutup, where sections of prose narrative were written on cards which were then shuffled to provide a narrative arrangement.

There is also accepting *chance intervention* by circumstances – when Marcel Duchamp's great work called *The Large Glass* was shattered in transit, he said, 'It is a lot better with the breaks, a hundred times better. It's the destiny of things.'

Dupain certainly spent much time exposed to the possibilities of what he called *luck of anticipation*. I am pretty sure he knew intuitively that if

At Newport – 1952

you hang about enough around the cavalcade of human activity which the beach presents, myriad possibilities will eventually present themselves. As Louis Pasteur said, 'Chance favours the prepared mind.'

Finally, there is the *found object*, an expression borrowed by Dupain from the Surrealist painters. In a sense, most photography is a found object: only the photograph where there is an elaborate arrangement or a posing of subject is not *found*.

By *found object* Dupain also meant those fortuitous encounters with the incongruous or bizarre in which he included finding nuns frolicking on a beach at Newport. Curiously, this idea has become a world-wide photographic cliché – nuns in any incongruous situation will inevitably be photographed!

Iconic status

As with many of his photographs, including those in this book, Dupain has captured recognisable Australian experiences which are 'subjects' not only of his time but for foreseeable times and which his brilliant craft has seized and, in some instances, elevated into iconic images.

They are empowered by his craft and his individual perception. Our appreciation of his craft comes after what literary critic Edmund Wilson described as a 'shock of recognition'.

A photograph which is finely crafted, which is repeatedly exposed to public view, and which speaks to a generation or to a national awareness can, after time, be adopted by media and by the public to become part of the communal visual memory.

This may be latent in the photograph until sufficient time has passed. An image somehow becomes alive when its relationship to history and public awareness has reached a certain critical point. Adoption of an image signifies that the image is alive with meanings and gives a sensation at each viewing: it is a form of ownership by a communal sensibility.

This, of course, is happening, or has happened, to *Sunbaker* and perhaps to *Bondi*, the *Meat queue*, and the pool-edge youths in *At Newport*.

And even if, with a further passing of time, generations other than ours see these photographs with a different time-focus – the nostalgic and the keyhole gaze having dissipated – these images will endure and, satisfyingly for Dupain, return to being more their art and less their subject.

Although, they will remain forever, as with all images – photographs of time itself.

Acknowledgments

Art in Australia, November 1935, a portfolio of Dupain's work.

Max Dupain Photographs, Ure Smith, Sydney, 1948, introduction by Hal Missingham, 'Some Notes About Photography' by Max Dupain.

Max Dupain, David Ell Press, Sydney, 1980, foreword by Peter Turner, appreciation by David Moore, essay by Gael Newton.

Max Dupain's Australia, Penguin Books, Melbourne, 1986, introduction by Max Dupain.

To Orange with Love, Max Dupain, Orange Regional Gallery, 1988.

Max Dupain's Australian Landscapes, Penguin Books, Melbourne 1988, introductions by Rosemary Dobson and Max Dupain.

Dupain's Sydney, Chapter & Verse, 1999, Sydney, Jill White, introduction by Zeny Edwards.

Dupain's Beaches, Chapter & Verse, 2000, Sydney, Jill White, introduction by Sebastian Smee.

ABC TV: Interview, *Arts Review*, 1991.

ABC TV: Max Dupain, *Arts and Entertainment*, 1990.

Unpublished essay on Dupain's early days, Claire Brown, 1994.

Conversations with Jill White and access to her archive of Max Dupain documents, tapes and other sources.

Conversations about Dupain's work with Joanna Logue.

FAMILY

A photographer's gaze almost inevitably turns first to his families – the one into which he or she was born and the one or more which he or she helps create. Dupain photographed the intimates of his families endlessly. He took many of his mother, Ena [below left].

He also photographed his father, George [opposite], a teacher of physical fitness who in his way pioneered the place of gymnasiums in our contemporary life.

His birth-family encouraged Dupain's ambitions to be a photographer – his grandmother and father bought him his first cameras. His grandmother also left him money when she died which helped him set up his first studio.

Dupain had two wives – his childhood companion and fellow photographer, Olive Cotton [below right], whom Dupain married when he was 28. The marriage produced no children and did not last long and after the war, aged 35, he married Diana Illingworth [p. 15] and they had a daughter and son, Danina [p. 15] and Rex [p. 14]. Rex has also become an accomplished photographer.

Dupain and his family followed the Australian tradition of the beach camping holiday – on the south and central NSW coasts – and these became some of his preferred photographic sites. Later in his life he returned as a photographer to his childhood family beach haunts.

The evidence suggests that Dupain was not perhaps a 'family man'. He had regrets about his relationship to his wife and children: in the introduction to his 1988 book *Australian Landscapes* he says of his second marriage, 'All in all I would never have wanted or asked for more satisfaction, but I do ask myself, have I reciprocated adequately', and in the book's dedication he thanks Diana for her patience and apologises for his 'insufferable single-mindedness'.

Zeny Edwards in her introduction to *Dupain's Sydney* records that Diana described Dupain as 'devil driven'. Edwards says that Dupain sought solitude through his photography, both in the darkroom and in his field work.

Above: Ena Dupain – n.d.
Above right: Olive Cotton – n.d.

Max's father in his library at Newport –1930s
George Zephirin Dupain (1881–1958) together with Max Cotton (a senior lecturer in physiology at Sydney University and Max Dupain's future father-in-law) created the Dupain Institute of Physical Education. George Dupain also wrote a number of books on physical education and nutrition, the most important being Exercise and Physical Fitness *(1948).*

Above: Rex's first waterfall – c. 1958
Taken at Minnamurra Falls on the south coast on a family holiday.

Opposite: Mother and child – 1952
Dupain's second wife, Diana, and their daughter Danina at Toowoon Bay.

NEW GUINEA

Although something of a pacifist, Dupain was not a conscientious objector and served in World War II as a photographer in the RAAF camouflage unit from 1941 until 1943. He said that he did not want to be a frontline war photographer as was his friend Damien Parer [p. 49].

Dupain was involved in aerial photography in PNG and surrounding islands and in Australia worked with the unit making camouflage netting to cover war equipment and buildings. The unit included artists and was commanded by Professor Dakin of the Zoology Department at the University of Sydney [p. 106].

The term camouflage comes from the French word *camoufler* meaning 'to blind or veil'. The ideas of recruiting artists, designers, architects and professional photographers into the camouflage units of the armed forces began in World War I.

The first *section de camouflage* in military history was established in 1915 by the French, under the command of an artist, and thereafter comparable units were used by the British and Americans and, to lesser extent, by the Germans. Wartime use of camouflage increased because of the beginning of surveillance by aircraft.

Many of Australia's best artists served in these units during World War II and were photographed by Dupain.

Dupain was sent to New Guinea when it was the battlefield for Australians and New Guineans fighting the Japanese invasion. Dupain described this wartime experience as 'the greatest external impression of my life – crowded with new forms and stimulating events'. It was from this wartime experience that he turned more towards documentary photography.

Right: Makeshift shower, New Guinea – 1943

Opposite: RAAF stand-down day,
Port Moresby – 1943
RAAF personnel enjoying a day off (usually a Sunday) sailing on Port Moresby Bay.

Opposite: RAAF officers, New Guinea – 1943

Bob Curtis and Clem Seal, Goodenough Island,
New Guinea – 1943
*Robert Emerson Curtis (1898–1996), an English-born artist,
studied in the USA before returning to Australia in 1928 when
he recorded the construction of the Sydney Harbour Bridge.
He served with Max and Clem Seal in New Guinea as Officer
in Charge of Camouflage there.*

Above: Up the mast – 1943

Opposite: Nimadao River, New Guinea – 1943

PORTRAITS

Except for the professional models we find here in Dupain's work, subjects who pose for a portrait experience unique discomforts and Dupain chooses to record it.

When those of us who are not professional models are being photographed we enter into a paradoxical unease – uncomfortably aware of ourselves and at the same time, conversely, losing a sense of ourselves. We are pinned in time like an insect unable to engage with our surroundings.

Not only are we disengaged from our authentic self, there is also an infringement of the cultural code of modesty. We are offering ourselves to be studied and perused as a subject worthy of being perused – either because of our beauty, or because of our status, or because of our celebrity or because of a 'special occasion' in our lives.

Being photographed infringes our cultural code of being 'unassuming'. All this comes out in the Dupain portraits of the painters Lloyd Rees [p. 31] and Joshua Smith [pp. 34, 35].

But with most of the other portraits here Dupain usually manages to capture his subjects when this ill-ease is not manifest or when they have succeeded in concealing it.

Some of these portraits are of professionals (not only models) who have been photographed many times and obviously have their ways of being 'present' while before the camera. Many of these were taken for Sydney Ure Smith's *The Home* magazine and for *Art in Australia*.

Of special interest in this group of portraits is Hal Salvage [left] who was the original model for the *Sunbaker* [right] which was taken in 1937 at Culburra Beach near Jervis Bay.

But perhaps it is not only the subject who is ill-at-ease during the taking of a portrait photograph.

Zeny Edwards in her essay on Dupain in *Dupain's Sydney* says that Dupain 'found it difficult doing portraits or being confronted by strangers…subjects are often depicted with their backs turned, eyes downcast…'.

And Dupain himself said, 'Why don't I like people? I wouldn't have a clue…'.

Hal Salvage – late 1930s
Harold (Hal) Salvage was a friend of Max Dupain; they shared a passion for rowing and often went on camping holidays. It was on one beach holiday on the south coast that Salvage became the model for Dupain's iconic photograph, Sunbaker.

Above: Sunbaker – 1937

Opposite: Chris Vandyke, Culburra Beach camp – 1937
Vandyke was a close friend who was also at the south coast Culburra Beach holiday when Dupain (at the age of 26) took Sunbaker.

Above: Francis Lymburner sketching, Bungan Beach – 1941
Francis Lymburner (1916–72), regarded as one of Australia's finest artists, came to Sydney in 1929 and was based in London from 1952 to 1964.

Opposite: Two girls at Bowral – 1939
Max's colleague and first wife, Olive Cotton (top) and Jean Lorraine, a favourite Dupain model (below).

Above: Jean Lorraine – 1937

Opposite: Greta – 1940

Athol Schmith – 1978
Schmith was a fashion photographer, once in partnership with
Helmut Newton. He married the model Patricia 'Bambi' Tuckwell.

Bambi Tuckwell – 1952
*Tuckwell was a well-known model in the 1950s and one of the founders
of the Mannequins' Association of Victoria.*

Above: Hal Missingham – early 1940s
Missingham left Australia in 1926 at the age of 20 to study in Europe like many of Dupain's friends and colleagues. He returned to Australia in 1940, worked as an artist and photographer, and later was the director of the Art Gallery of NSW until 1971.

Opposite: Lloyd Rees – 1979
Rees (1895–1988) was one of Australia's most widely respected landscape painters. Born in Yeronga, Brisbane, he held his first one-man show in 1918 and had numerous exhibitions around Australia and in Britain, the United States, Europe and Asia. His awards included the Silver Medal at the Paris Exposition (1937) and the Wynne Prize (1950 and 1982).

Opposite: Russell Drysdale – 1950s
Drysdale (1912–81) studied at the Julian Ashton Art School in Sydney and the Slade School, London and became one of the leaders of Australian modernist painting.

Above: Bill Dobell, Bankstown – early 1940s
William Dobell (1899–1970) was Australia's most talented and successful portrait artist although his work also included figures and landscapes. Dobell's 'Portrait of the artist' [Joshua Smith – pp. 34, 35] was awarded the 1943 Archibald Prize. Many considered it a caricature and thus not eligible for the portrait prize and the controversy ended with a famous trial.

Above: Joshua Smith – early 1940s
A highly respected painter, Smith (1905–95) was the subject of the disputed 1943 Archibald Prize winning portrait by William Dobell. The painter William Dargie supported Dobell, and commented 'How dare they call that picture of Smith caricatured? I saw him in Sydney one day. He was caricatured in himself.'

Opposite: Joshua Smith with camouflage nets, Bankstown – 1942
William Dobell and Smith had been friends since 1939 when they served as camouflage painters in the army.

Above: Marie Rosenfeld – 1937
The actress Marie Rosenfeld starred in Charles Chauvel's 1933 film
In the Wake of the Bounty *with Errol Flynn.*

Above: Leon Gellert – 1937
Co-editor of the influential magazine Home *in the 1920s and 1930s,
Gellert took part in the Gallipoli landings and is acclaimed as an essayist
and one of Australia's greatest war poets. After World War II he became a
journalist on* The Sydney Morning Herald. *Norman Lindsay illustrated
his epic poem,* The Isle of San.

Opposite: Jean Bellette – c. 1936
*Bellette (1908–91), a painter, was part of the Sydney Group, founded
in 1945 and active until about 1957. Their intention was to reverse what
they saw as the decline of the conservative New South Wales Society
of Artists.*

Above: Margaret Preston – n.d.
Margaret Preston (1875–1963) was one of Australia's foremost artists, celebrated for her oils and prints of Australian flora and fauna.

Opposite: Norman Lindsay – 1936
The painter Norman Lindsay's (1879–1970) writings had an influence on the young Dupain but his parents discouraged this, probably because of the controversy that surrounded Lindsay and his views of sexuality.

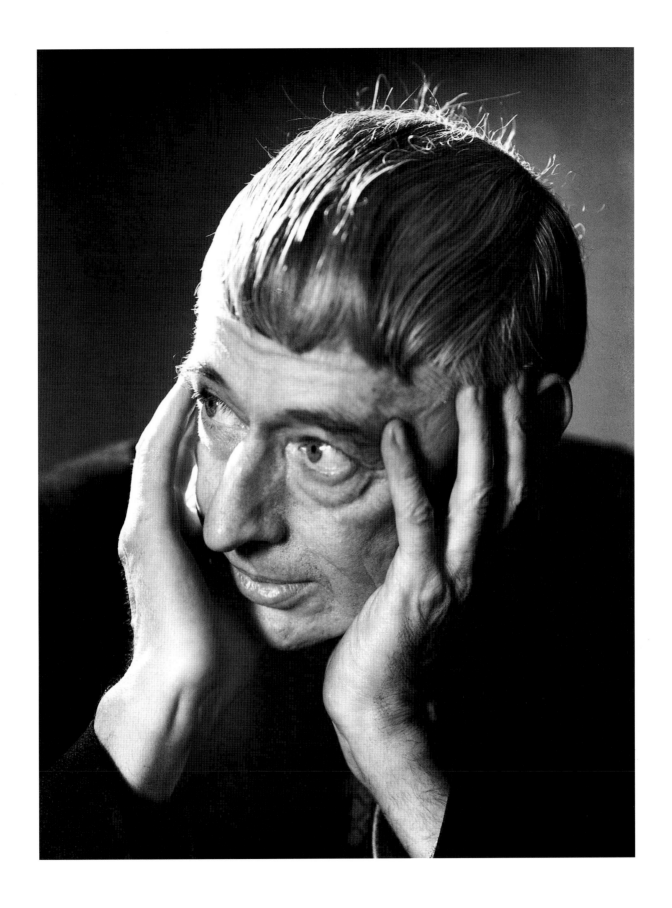

Above: Douglas Glass for *Art & Design* – 1948
Glass (1901–78) had a portrait and fashion photography studio in London with Gordon Crocker.

Above right: Marie Rosenfeld – c. 1936

Opposite: Eleanor Dark
Eleanor Dark (1901–85) is an important figure in Australian literary history. She published ten novels, one of which, The Timeless Land, became a best-seller in Australia and the USA and was later made into a popular television series. Eleanor's novels were popular, sometimes controversial and experimental, and they reflected Australian history and culture in a way that was unusual for the time at which they were published (1932–77).

Above: June Dally-Watkins and flower – n.d.
In the 1950s June Dally-Watkins was Australia's first 'supermodel' and founded Australia's first modelling school in 1950. The school trained eight winners of the Miss Australia award. Dally-Watkins subsequently opened a successful modelling agency.

Opposite: Eugene Goossens – n.d.
The British-born Sir Eugene Goossens (1893–1962) was appointed as Chief Conductor of the Sydney Symphony Orchestra and Director of the NSW Conservatorium of Music in 1947. In March 1957 Goossens was caught trying to smuggle into Australia banned books, ritual masks and '1,166 pornographic photographs'. Sir Eugene was fined and he returned to England.

Gropius and Seidler, Turramurra – 1954

Harry Seidler, Walter and Ilse Gropius at Rose Seidler
House, Turramurra – 1954
*Walter Gropius (1883–1969) founded the Bauhaus, one of the
most influential architecture and design schools of the twentieth
century. Driven from Germany by the rise of National Socialism,
he eventually settled in Boston, where he taught at Harvard and*
*MIT. Harry Seidler was born in Vienna in 1923, studied with
Walter Gropius at Harvard and settled in Australia in 1948.
He is recognised as one of Australia's leading architects of the
modern movement and the first architect in Australia to fully
express the principles of the Bauhaus.*

THE PARER ALBUM

These photographs serve both as a personal interlude to this book and, at the same time, a touching glimpse of wartime Australia.

Dupain created the album of 45 photographs – titled *A few shots from home* – for his friend, renowned war cinematographer Damien Parer (1912–44) [p. 49] for Christmas, 1940.

Parer was an outstanding cinematographer, famous for dramatic footage of Australian soldiers in the Middle East and New Guinea during World War II. He had worked for a time with Max Dupain before turning to cinema.

At the time the album was sent to him, Parer was an official war photographer in the Western Desert near Bardia, Libya with the 6th Division of the Australian Army. He was later killed while filming in 1944 on Peleliu, a Pacific Island, as he walked backwards photographing American Marines going into action.

The commentary in the album is in Dupain's handwriting. Ten of the photographs are of attractive female models – perhaps intended for passing around among the troops.

The first two photographs in this section from the album are of Dupain and Olive Cotton, his newly-wedded wife, with the playful lines "Fancy a sweet innocent thing like this marrying a –" opposite the Cotton photograph, and "bastard like him" opposite his own picture.

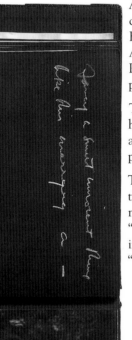

Marie Cotter – 1937
She was later married to photographer and cinematographer Damien Parer.

The third photograph is of Marie Cotter (who later married Parer) with the line "Boy! oh Boy!" [above].

The photograph on the left is of Jean Lorraine [pp. 25, 26], a friend of Olive Cotton and a favourite model of Dupain's, who was well-known to Parer. The inscription reads "New outdoor portrait of Jean Lorraine (Mrs McInerney)". Jean was married to John McInerney whose brother Ross was Olive Cotton's second husband. Jean's second husband was an American and she became a photographer and journalist in the US (including the Panama Canal zone for many years). In 2003 she was living in Richmond, Virginia.

Finally, they included another photograph of themselves with the line "Merry Xmas from us both".

Typically for the times, the photographs are glued to heavy black photographic mounting-paper and bound together with album cord. The Mitchell Library in Sydney holds the album.

Damien Parer – June 1944

NUDES

As I have said in the introduction, the nudes from our parents' time give a keyhole view (which never really satisfies) for our childish curiosity about what our parents were like naked and when involved in physical intimacy.

Nudes – actual, painted, or photographed – are eternally fascinating but especially the female nude. As the title of the famous painting by Gustave Courbet *The Origin of the World* says (a painting of the female genitalia looking up the female body from the knees), the female nude represents the source of us all – male and female – and because of this fundamental connection we are universally and insatiably drawn to it.

Dupain's nudes in this volume depict only one man and he is in a classical discus thrower pose [p. 55].

His female nudes reminded me of those that were published in the 1930s and 1940s in men's magazines such as *Man*. To avoid censorship, the nudes were presented as 'art photography' – dressed up with a couplet of verse or a title such as 'Coming of Spring' and with the nude holding a sprig of blossom, or with blossom covering the nipples and genitals.

They were called nude 'studies'…as if one were looking at them essentially to study the history of the nude? Photographic technique? All nudes in those days were erotic, in that, given the social context of extreme sexual inhibition, of reserve, censorship and silence about sexuality, any glimpse of the sexually concealed became arousing.

I asked Jill White whether Dupain ever published his nudes in such magazines but she wasn't sure; however he did publish them in the mainstream magazine *Home* in the 1930s as 'studies'.

He did take many nude photographs. His early studio partner Reg Johnson was described by Dupain as having a primary photographic concern: 'pretty girls and more pretty girls. There was no choice if you were going to pay the rent'.

The pole shot [p. 54] by historical accident reminds me of the 'exotic' pole dancers in some clubs where nude girls dance suggestively around a chrome-plated pole. It is difficult to know from where this particular Dupain image comes.

I have a special connection with *The little nude* [opposite] which is of Olive Cotton – Dupain's first wife – taken when she was in her twenties. The photograph was used to illustrate the first paperback edition of my novel *Grand Days*.

It is a perfect example of what Dupain strove for – the relegation of 'subject' – where the light and composition and body form are very close to being 'everything'. The subject is almost secondary. But still sensuality creeps in as our eyes run down the spine to the crevice of the buttocks.

Nude study [p. 53] is closer to the classic sensual pose of abandon or surrender with the head thrown back although this also probably served the purpose of concealing the model's identity in those more moralistic times.

Opposite: The little nude – 1938
The model was Dupain's first wife, Olive Cotton.

Above: Nude with shadow – 1930s

Opposite: Nudy study – 1930s

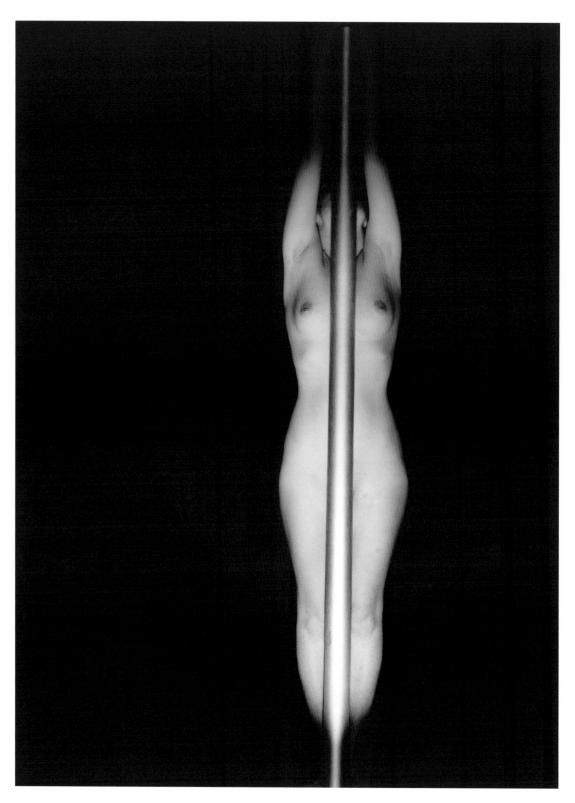

Above: Nude with pole – 1930s
Opposite: Discus – 1937

Above: Nude in grass – 1939

Opposite: Jean with wire mesh – 1937

WORKERS

Dupain took most of these photographs of Australians at work as institutional commissions: they were not subjects he would have naturally sought. The assignments came from places such as the Colonial Sugar Refining Company Limited and the Department of Information which commissioned him to do a series called 'Girls at Work' in 1946. In the same year the City of Newcastle engaged him to take the photographs for a book celebrating the city's 150th year.

There is a studied, professional formalism in most of the compositions where he works with the vertical [pp. 62, 63] and with lines receding to a point [pp. 60, 64] – all worked up from the sites by Dupain through arrangement of subject and camera angle where he lays in his verticals, horizontals and so on like a carpenter.

But two photographs stand out as being more complex and almost inexplicable in their power. The first is *Sandwich Girl* [opposite] where the personality of the girl is striking in its intensity. The intensity comes from the bulk and sheen of her hair and her bright facial expression, the energy of her body tautness, especially in the extended partial grip of her right hand, her main working hand.

I consider this as another contender for iconic status along with *Sunbaker* and *Meat queue*.

A strong sense of 'another time' also now exudes from the photograph, perhaps inviting us to be charmed by the illusion that in the stance and expression of the *Sandwich Girl* we glimpse a time of greater simplicity, of fabled innocence, of heightened vitality.

But perhaps the most compositionally complex photograph is that of the resting motorbike cowboys on the Queensland cattle station [p. 69].

When I look at this photograph my eye alights first on the Honda insignia of the bike in the foreground, then the bike itself which takes me back and forward along the body of the bike, that is, across the foreground. My eye then moves directly back into the photograph to the four fanned forked branches of the tree in the middle ground, then across to the parked bike pointing to the background, taking me into the endless scrub wilderness where the men had been working. Only then does my eye come down to the men resting casually under the tree. And only

Above: Postwar postie – 1946

Opposite: Sandwich girl – 1946

incidentally does my eye observe the nose of a ute or four-wheel drive in the left of the centre background, working in the photograph as a blocking or framing 'shape', not as a feature of the work scene.

The photograph directs the eye with complex decisiveness giving the image a persistent aliveness.

Above: Australian Wire Rope workers, Newcastle – early 1940s

Opposite: Aircraft maintenance worker, Newcastle – 1940s

Opposite: Up a ladder, Cane-ite factory, Pyrmont – mid-1950s
A steam-heated platen press was used to convert wet mats of wood pulp to
'Masonite' – a type of hardboard sheet. The factory was on the eastern side
of the old Glebe Island Bridge (now replaced by the Anzac Bridge).

Above: Old Wunderlich factory at Rose Hill – 1975

Above: Burwood Colliery, Hunter Valley – 1947

Opposite: Miners drilling – 1947

Above: Cane farmer, Mackay region, Queensland – 1950s

Opposite: Young cane farm worker, Mackay region, Queensland – 1950s

Above: Stockyards, North Queensland – 1980
*This photograph and the two following were taken
on CSR stations in North Queensland.*

Opposite: Smoko, North Queensland – 1980s

Above: Shearing, North Queensland – 1978

Opposite: Curious boy – 1958

WINE MAKING

Given Australia's passion for wine these photographs take us back to one of the vineyards where it all began and to a man to whom we owe some of this passion – Maurice O'Shea [p. 77].

The vineyards are in the Hunter Valley of New South Wales owned by McWilliam's and the photographs were taken in 1951.

O'Shea was an Australian who, under the influence of his mother, went to France as a teenager just after World War I to study wine making. His parents at the time owned what is now known as the Mount Pleasant vineyard, a name given to it by O'Shea after his return from France. Wines are still produced under the Mount Pleasant label by McWilliam's.

In some ways, O'Shea as a winemaker resembled Dupain in his technical conservatism. Throughout his professional wine-making life, O'Shea preferred the traditional wine-making equipment and the techniques which he had learned in France.

In an essay on O'Shea, Nick Chlebnikowski says that, 'He used to believe that if the crop were clean and the wine maker knew his job, he could usually make a better wine than could be produced by more mechanised processes, simply because the wine maker was closer to his wine, watched over it more studiously, became altogether much more intimate with it in all its stages'.

O'Shea grew Semillon, black and white Pinot, Traminer, Picpoule, Aucerot, Rhine Riesling, Montils, Madeira, Hermitage and Cabernet Sauvignon.

O'Shea was a great eccentric and evidently a great cook. Chlebnikowski points out that '...his roast bandicoot was, if not renowned, at least startling. Even more startling was his starling pie. But his Hunter River wild duck, casseroled in Mount Pleasant Hermitage, with mushrooms, would have made any chef proud'. Legend has it that O'Shea cooked on a kerosene stove. He had no gas, no electricity.

The Dupain images evoke these more traditional wine making times.

Right: Children at O'Shea's Winery, Pokolbin – 1951

Opposite: Grape harvesters, Pokolbin – 1951

Unloading wine barrels, Pokolbin – 1951

Three men on wine press – 1951

Cleaning wine casks, Pokolbin – 1951

Maurice O'Shea, winemaker, Pokolbin – 1951

AUSTRALIANS

While in my main introduction I may have tried to elevate nostalgia to an aesthetically respectable position from which to view Dupain's work at this time in history, it does have some companion sensibilities which may not be as intellectually defensible.

These are the sensibilities or more precisely *sensations* of sentimentality and the romanticising of the past.

The photograph *Bankstown boys don't cry* [p. 5] perhaps illustrates this best but others in this section invite us in the direction of sentimentality, for example, *Little girl in a thunderstorm* [p. 80], *Ice cream at Townsville* [p. 82], *Black and white, Cairns* [p. 83], and *Coolah landscape* [p. 87].

I do not think it is always the fault of the photographs. In fact, it shows how many obstacles viewers themselves can place in the way of 'seeing' a photograph, obstacles which spring up like tropical growth from our cultural conditioning to obscure the photograph. It could, I suppose, be argued that these are all legitimate ways of seeing, part of the plurality of responses which an image can trigger, especially a powerfully presented image.

Australia has folk sentimentality about the urchin and the 'larrikin' (although this is I suspect more a literary sentimentality) and like *Bankstown boys don't cry*, *Little Aussie* [p. 81] is awash with it, or at least I can see that it invites these cultural linkages and the flossy pleasures they give. But the urchin, as subject, also links legitimately to the universal appeal of, and our natural curiosity about, the young.

The urchin – the mischievous, raggedly dressed child, usually a street child – has been a favourite of photographers since the beginning of photography.

Nearly all the great names have photographed urchins – Robert Doisneau, Henri Cartier-Bresson, Sabine Weiss, Brassaï, way back to Jacob Riis in the 1890s and even earlier with Humbert de Molard's *Two Boys* taken about 1848 (only about ten years after what is seen as the beginning of photography).

Some of the photographs in this section invite other related sentiments about our forebears – as being the true battlers, stalwarts, survivors, independent spirits and a fear that we are not made of the same stuff – 'giants walked the land then'.

Regardless of Dupain's intention, photography sometimes invites us to savour these sentimental fallacies and to incorporate the photographs into our legend making.

Above: Street scene – 1960s

Opposite: Portrait of a boy in sunlight – 1936

Above: Little girl in a thunderstorm – 1949
*A thunderstorm followed by a rainbow during a family
portrait session caused the anxiety in this child.*

Opposite: Little Aussie – 1942

Ice cream at Townsville – 1943

Black and white, Cairns – 1960

Above: Grafton cyclist – n.d.

Opposite: Signalman Jack with poor lame dog, Orange – 1988

Above: Coolah landscape – 1959

Opposite: Hot day, Roma, Queensland – 1980

Depression – 1938

Domain dosser – 1938

Above: Bus queue, The Spit – 1946   Opposite: At the show – 1940

On the ferry – n.d.

Sightseers in a bus – 1956
Visitors to the new AOR refinery site at Kurnell.

Tired soldier in train, North Queensland – 1943

Passengers in North Queensland train – 1943

Bus shelter, Toowoon Bay – 1960s

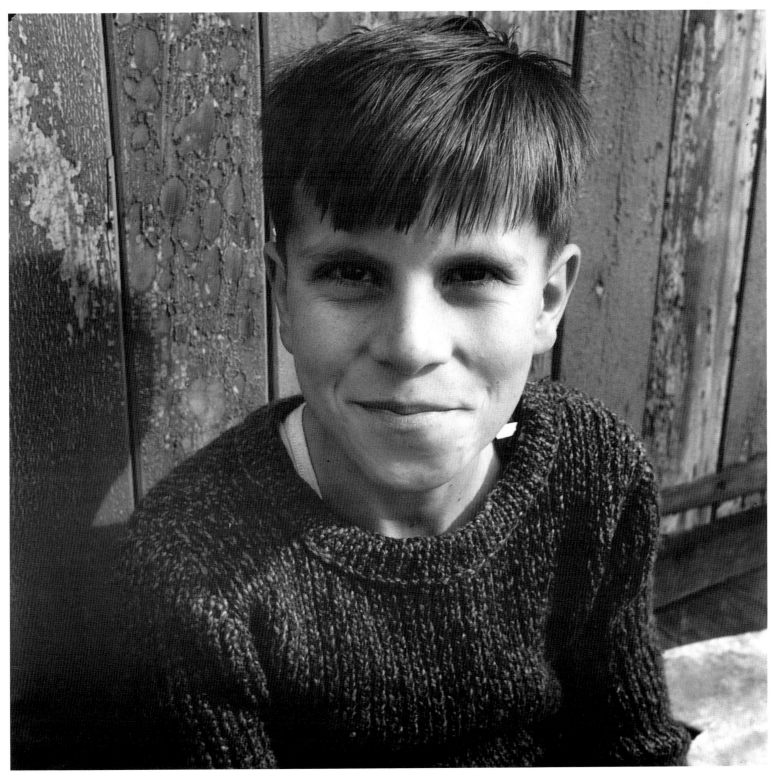

Smiling boy at Glebe – 1939
This portrait was commissioned to send to the boy's father,
a soldier who had just been sent to the front.

Typing class at Miss Hale's academy, Sydney – n.d.

Petty's Hotel, Sydney, 6 pm – 1941
This hotel at 1 York Street, Sydney, lasted for over a century before becoming the home of the Red Cross Blood Bank. Max's studio was just opposite at 49 Clarence Street.
Until 1955, pubs in NSW closed at 6pm. The limited time after work to drink was called the 'six o'clock swill'.

Crows Nest Fruit market – 1950

Roadside store – 1940s

Lifesavers – 1940s

Deck chairs for hire – *c.* 1943

Above: Jesus saves – n.d.

Opposite: Chickens for sale, Little Collins Street, Melbourne – 1946

DARWIN TRIP

Dupain entered the war in 1942 as a camouflage photographer for the Department of Home Security after the Japanese bombing of Darwin and Broome in 1941 had brought World War II to Australia and with it great upheaval.

In the Pacific the Japanese advance had been equally dramatic, reaching Lae and Salamaua in New Guinea by March 1942. This was seen as the first stage before a Japanese advance on Australia.

The Japanese then attempted an overland attack against Port Moresby. Australian militia troops and battalions of the 7th Division were sent to Port Moresby and met the Japanese forces on the Kokoda Trail where they were eventually repelled after coming very close to Port Moresby. Japanese units continued to resist strongly in the extremely difficult terrain adjoining the coast until mid-January 1943.

After training at Bankstown, Dupain and another camouflage officer, Gus Dignam, were assigned to the RAAF and ordered to Darwin. They took a train to Adelaide and from there travelled by train to Alice Springs, living in a motor van lashed to a flat-bed rail car.

While waiting in Alice Springs for their commanding officer, Professor Dakin, Dupain explored and photographed the countryside '...as coastal inhabitants, we were totally unprepared for it. Great rearing cliffs of red granite arching into pure cobalt and white trunked eucalypts spouting from their flanks...'.

Dupain spent a year in Darwin photographing the countryside and designing and building camouflage screens to cover oil tank installations. Darwin had been badly damaged by the bombing in 1941 and Dupain found it 'a patched-up military town and fortunately for the sanity of all, a little skulduggery provided beer in plenty...'.

In these photographs, Dupain gives a glimpse of life in the outback on the way to Darwin during those war years.

Above: Professor Dakin en route to Darwin – 1943
Professor William John Dakin (1883–1950) held the Derby Chair of Zoology, University of Liverpool from 1921 to 1928, before becoming Challis Professor of Zoology, University of Sydney, 1928 to 1948.

Opposite: Bush kitchen, Ti Tree Well, Northern Territory – 1943

Above: Roy Dalgarno, Darwin – 1943
*Dalgarno (1910–2001) was an artist noted for his social realism;
like many artists, he served as a camouflage officer in World War II.*

Opposite: Back yard, Ti Tree Well, Northern Territory – 1943

Above: Max Dupain in Darwin – 1943

Opposite: Stopover on way to Darwin – 1943

BIOGRAPHICAL TIME LINE
FOR MAXWELL SPENCER DUPAIN

YEAR	AGE	
1911		born Maxwell Spencer Dupain in Ashfield, an inner Western suburb of Sydney
1924	13	is given his first camera, a Box Brownie
1927	16	fails Leaving Certificate at Sydney Grammar – grandmother buys him a more advanced 'vest pocket' camera
1928	17	fails Leaving Certificate for second time but is given the Carter Memorial School Prize for Productive Use of Spare Time for an exhibition of landscape photographs
1929	18	his father gives him a Thornton Pickard Half Plate camera – begins work for Smith & Julius as an apprentice photographer to Cecil Bostock and studies photography at the East Sydney Technical College and Julian Ashton Art School
1934	23	sets up his first studio on the corner of Bond and Hamilton Streets in Sydney – breaks with the Pictoralist School of photography – begins nude photographs
1935	24	*Art in Australia* magazine publishes a portfolio of his work which is partly Man Ray influenced
1936	25	buys his first car, a Chevrolet roadster
1937	26	*Soul of A City*, illustrated by Dupain, edited by O. Ziegler – *Sunbaker* images photographed
1938	27	first one-person show at the University of Sydney – *Little nude* (of Olive Cotton) taken
1939	28	marries Olive Cotton – takes *Bondi* which is to become an iconic Australian photograph
1941	30	moves studio to 49 Clarence Street and amalgamates with Hartland & Hyde, process engravers – World War II service in the camouflage unit – separates from Olive Cotton
1943	32	To New Guinea with camouflage unit and later back in Australia with the Department of Information (until 1947)
1946	35	marries Diana Illingworth – photographs the iconic *Meat queue*
1948	37	*Max Dupain Photographs*, Ure Smith, Sydney, introduction by Hal Missingham, 'Some Notes About Photography' by Max Dupain, in which the first *Sunbaker* is published

YEAR	AGE	
1950	39	daughter Danina born
1954	43	son Rex born – resigns from Institute of Photographic Illustrators and forms a group called 6 Photographers with Gordon Andrews, Kerry Dundas, Hal Missingham, Axel Poignant and David Potts – becomes interested in architectural photography
1955	44	first exhibition by the 6 Photographers at David Jones Art Gallery
1958	47	Jill White begins work as an assistant to Dupain (until 1960)
1970	59	Jill White returns to work as his assistant and does so until his death in 1992
1975	64	*Sunbaker* photograph as we know it appears as poster image for the first Dupain retrospective at the Australian Centre for Photography in Sydney
1978	67	spends two weeks in Paris photographing the new Australian embassy designed by Harry Seidler
1980	69	*Max Dupain*, David Ell Press, Sydney, foreword by Peter Turner, appreciation by David Moore, essay by Gael Newton
1982	71	OBE for services to photography
1983	72	made an Honorary Fellow of the Royal Australian Institute of Architects
1986	75	*Max Dupain's Australia*, Penguin Books, introduction by Max Dupain
1988	77	*Max Dupain's Australian Landscapes*, Penguin Books, introductions by poet Rosemary Dobson and Max Dupain
1991	80	retrospective at NSW State Library and Australian National Gallery – *Max Dupain*, Print Room Press, Sydney, introduction by Jill White, tribute by David Moore, limited edition to celebrate his 80th birthday
1992	81	Companion of the Order of Australia for service to the visual arts, dies in his sleep in hospital